book

This ~~sausage~~ belongs to

D1386246

5430000512622 1

It's MY Sausage
An original concept by author Alex Willmore
© Alex Willmore 2019

Illustrated by Alex Willmore
© Alex Willmore

MAVERICK ARTS PUBLISHING LTD
Studio 11, City Business Centre, 6 Brighton Road, Horsham,
West Sussex, RH13 5BB, +44 (0)1403 256941
© Maverick Arts Publishing Limited
Published September 2019

A CIP catalogue record for this book

is available at the British Library.

ISBN 978-1-84886-429-0
www.maverickbooks.co.uk

Maverick publishing

Lerner

It's MY Sausage

ALEX WILLMORE

To my mischievous kitties,
Osker and Markley

There are five of us
but just **one** sausage.

It's MY sausage!

I saw it first and
I'm saving it for later.

So don't even think about taking <u>my</u> sausage!

Step away from MY sausage!

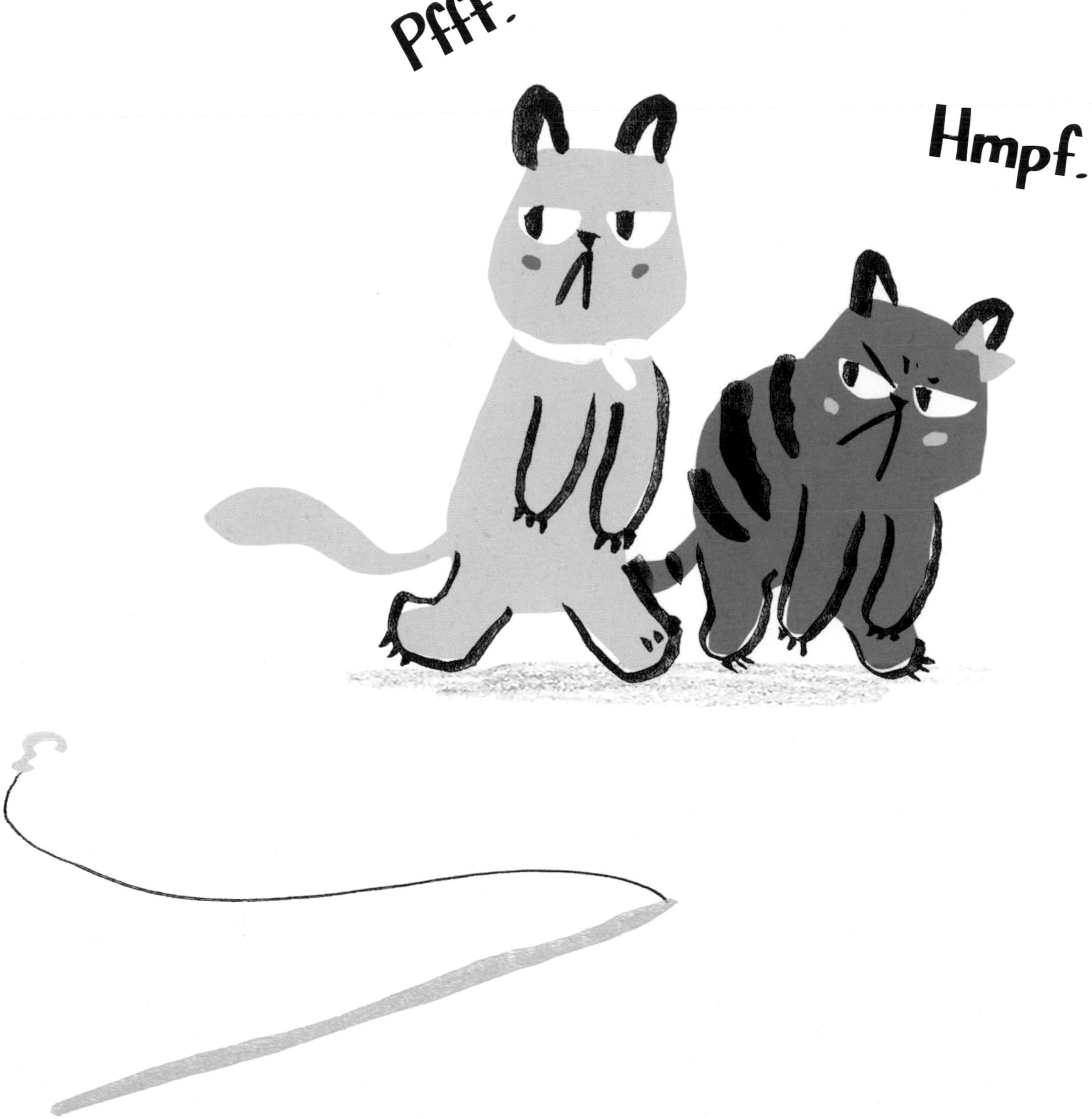
Pffft.
Hmpf.

Yummy!

Scrummy!

Sausage...

Snip

SPLAT!

You can all just stop it right now.

Because this
sausage is mine...

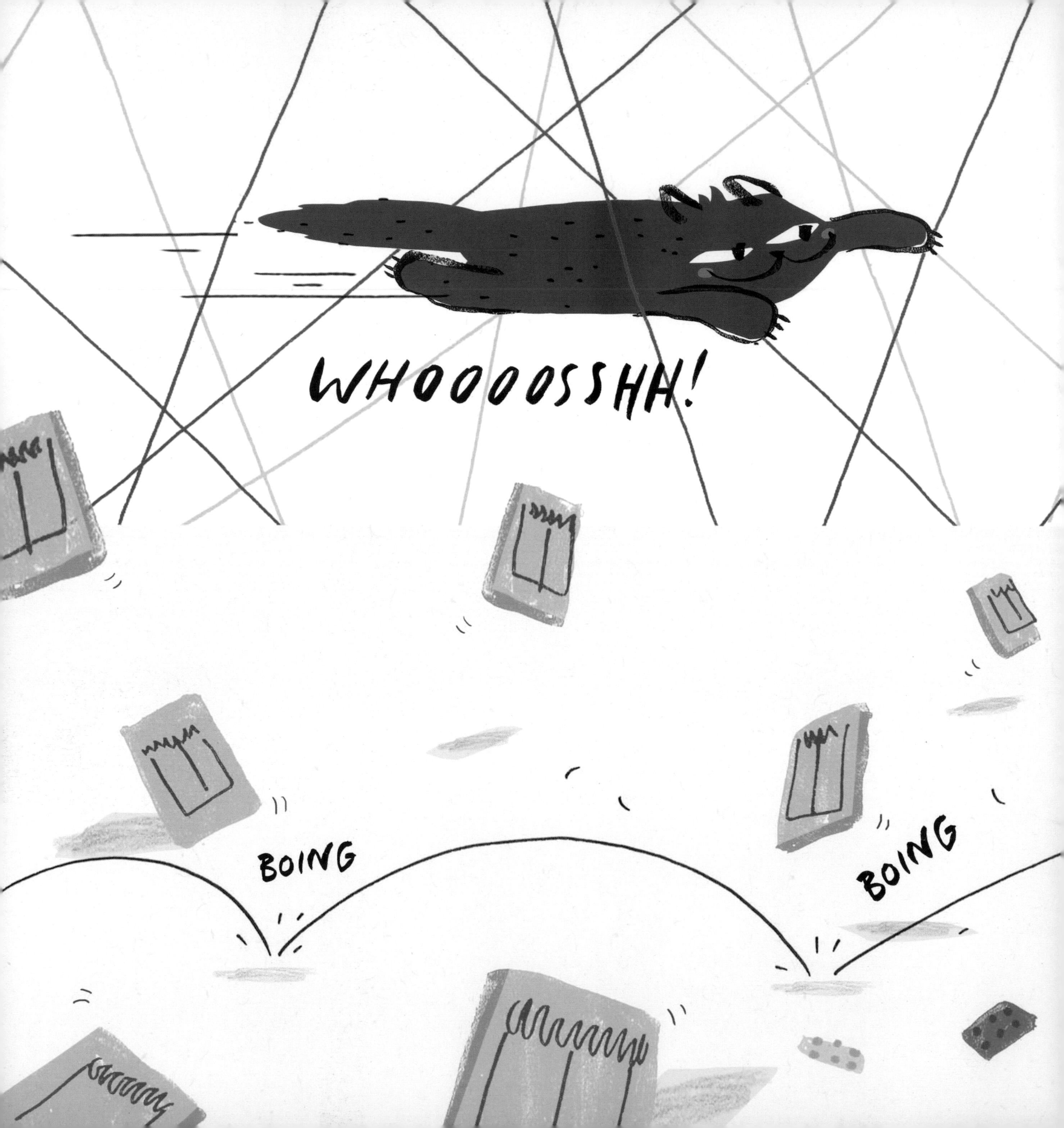
WHOOOOOSSHH!
BOING
BOING

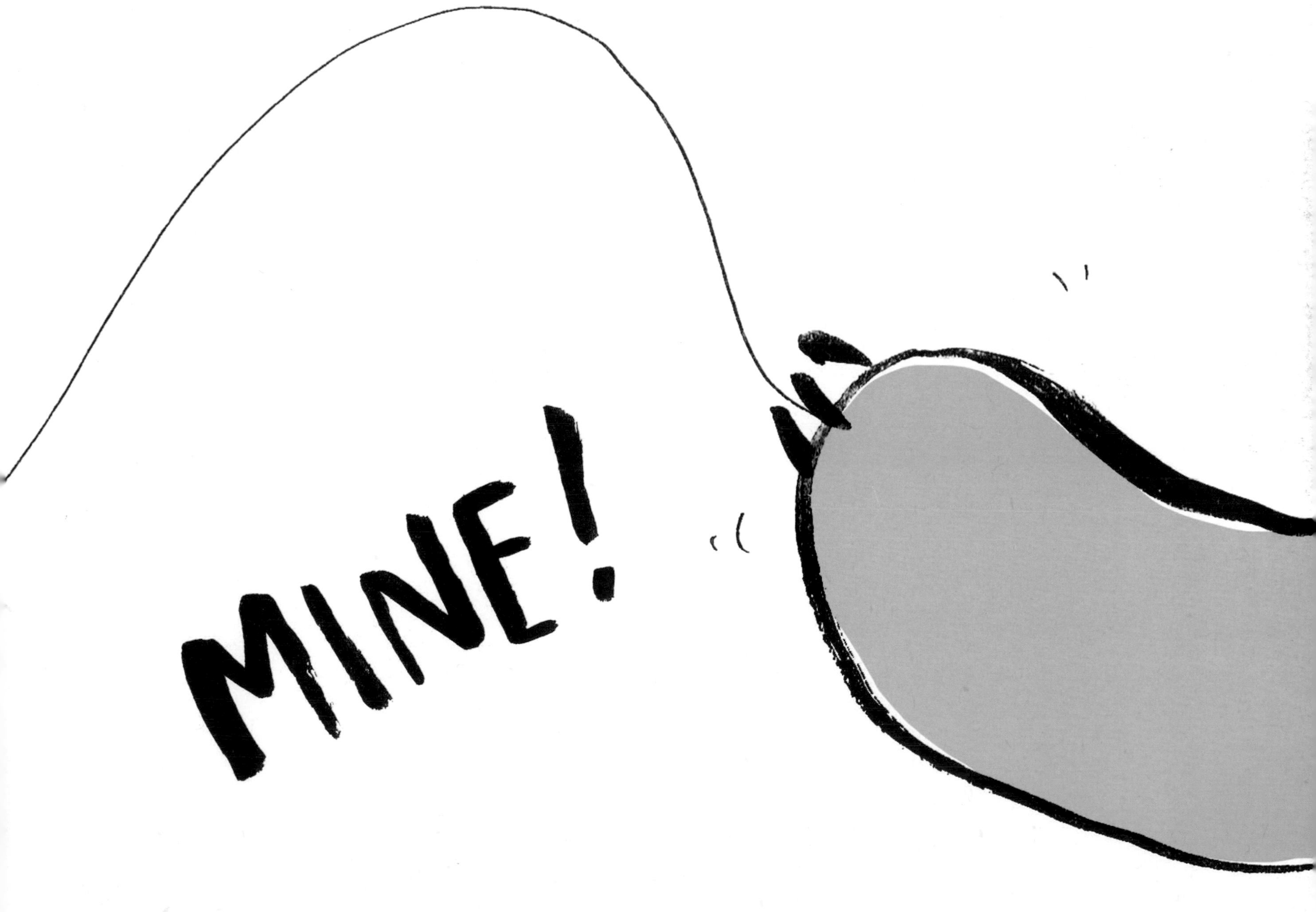
MINE!

It's MY sausage!

Mine Mine Mine Mine Mine...

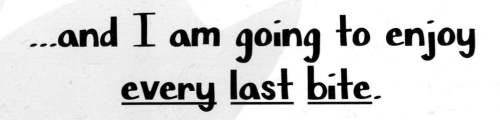

...and I am going to enjoy
<u>every last bite</u>.

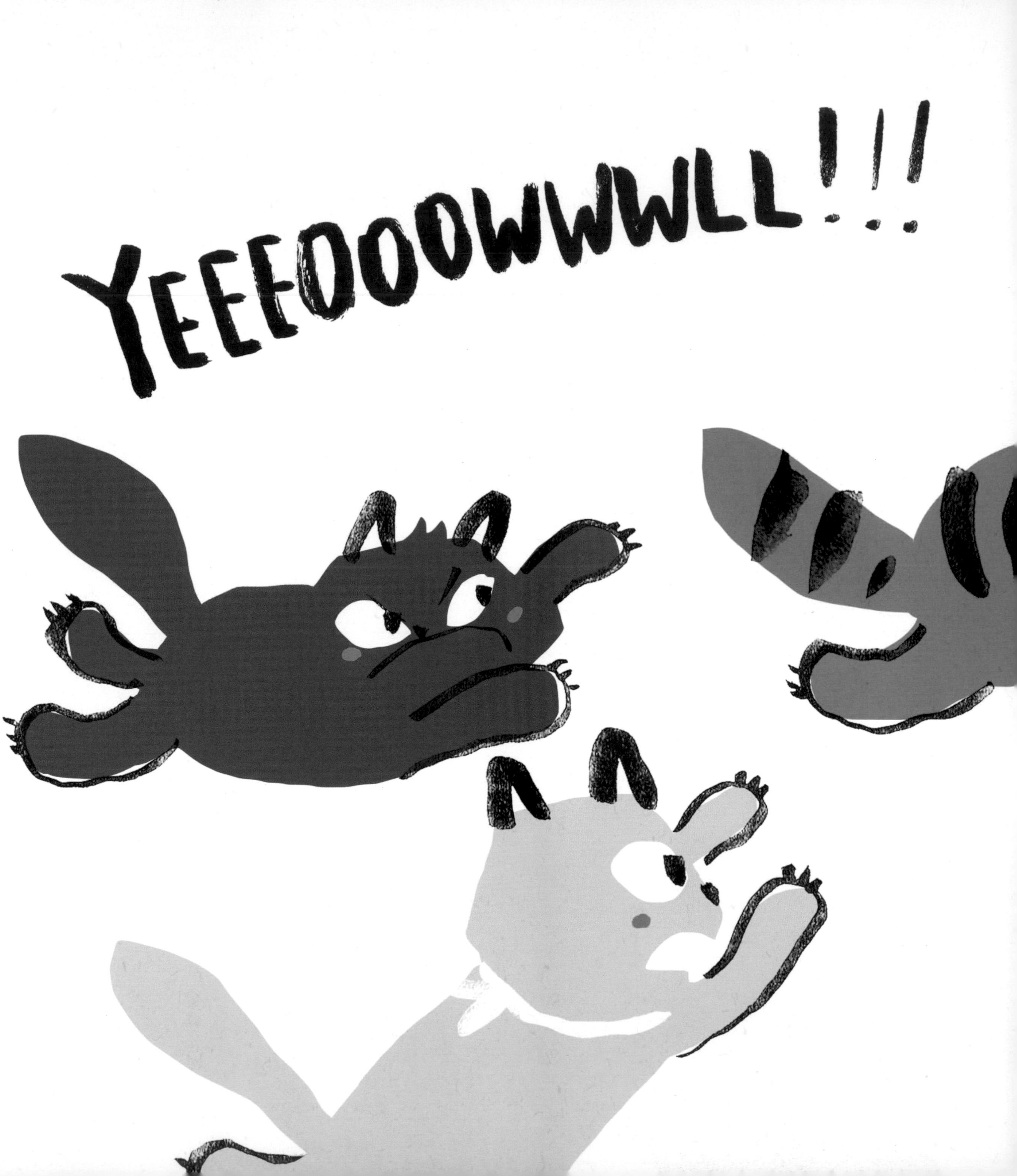
YEEEOOOWWWLL!!!

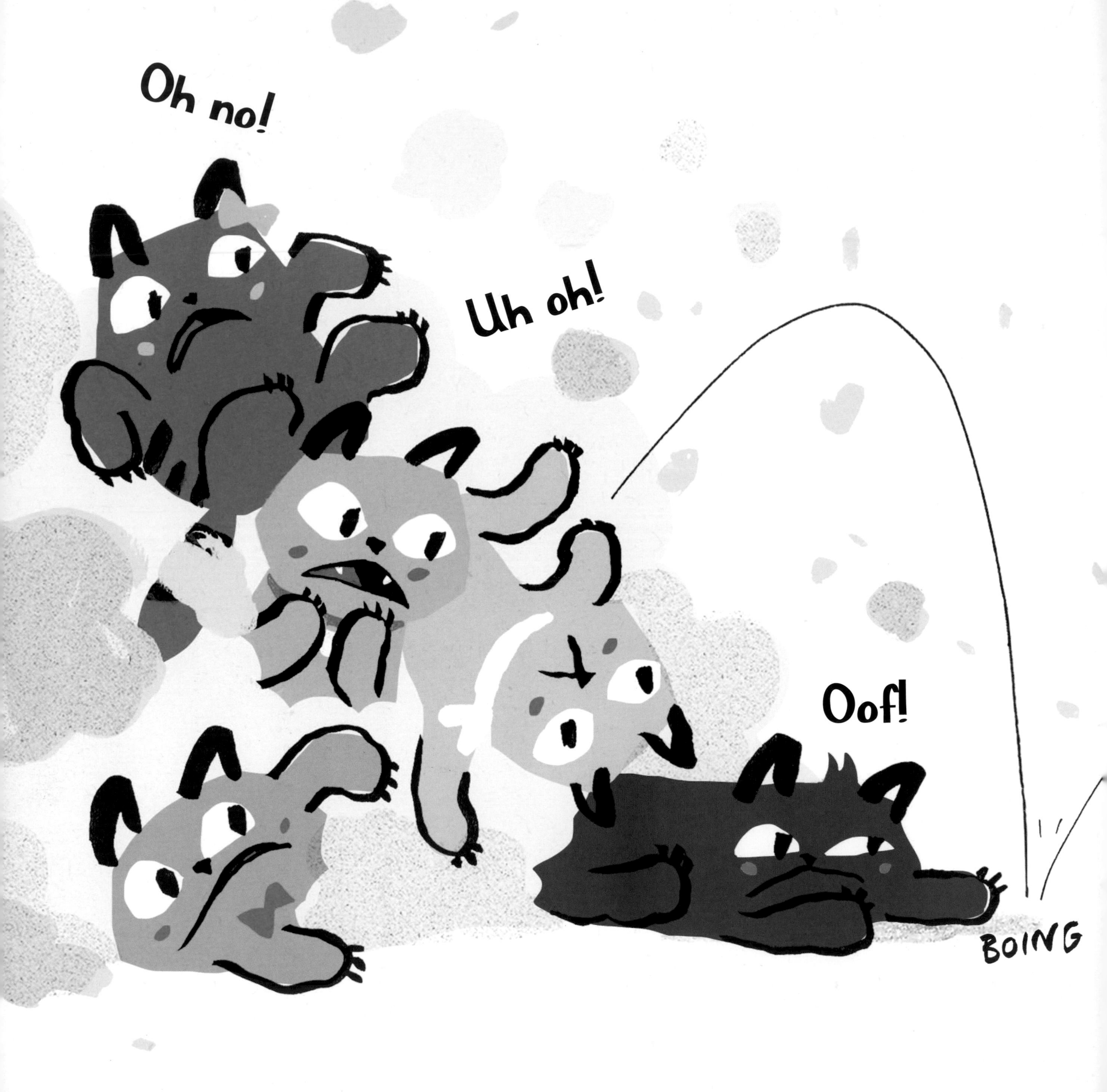

Oh no!
Uh oh!
Oof!
BOING